A JOURNEY THROUGH TIME

VULCA
THE ETRUSCAN

Published in the United States of America by
Oxford University Press, Inc.
198 Madison Avenue
New York, NY 10016
Oxford is a registered trademark of Oxford University Press, Inc.
ISBN 0-19-521506-0

© 1998 Istituto Geografico De Agostini S.p.A., Novara
English text © 1998 British Museum Press
Published in Great Britain by British Museum Press
Published in Italy as *A Spasso Con ... Vulca l'Etrusco*
Printed in Italy by Officine Grafiche, Novara, 1998
Illustrations: Roberta Angeletti
Text: Beatrice Masini

VULCA
THE ETRUSCAN

by Roberta Angeletti

Oxford University Press
New York

One sunny morning, Robbie and his dog Pip were strolling happily along the path to the Necropolis. It was a secret and mysterious place, high up on a hill, with lots of open space for playing ball. They always went there when they wanted some freedom. Robbie put his ball down on the ground, then, with a huge kick, he sent it flying out of sight.

On the other side of the hill, Vulca the Etruscan was sitting alone, playing his flute and listening to the soft murmur of the sea. Vulca loved the Necropolis too. He had lived there a long, long time and had seen many things, so he was not at all surprised when he saw the brightly colored ball flying through the air.

"Where's my ball gone?" wondered Robbie. "Go and find it, Pip!" he shouted. But they couldn't find it anywhere. Some-one must have picked it up, thought Robbie. He peered down a dark, narrow stairway leading underground. "Perhaps it's in there! Let's go down!" But when they reached the bottom all they found was a funny wooden thing.

Robbie looked around. "Where are we?" he asked.
But Pip didn't answer. He couldn't open his mouth because
of the wooden thing, which he had picked up and was now
holding tight between his teeth. If I can't have the ball, he
thought, at least I can keep this stick. But it wasn't a stick.
It was a pair of old, old pipes — Etruscan pipes!

Robbie and Pip were standing in a little square room. There was no light, but their eyes soon got used to the dark. There were so many things to look at! The walls of the room were covered with brightly colored paintings. Some were of huge vases, so beautifully painted that they seemed real.

High up on one wall two leopards were glaring at each other with fierce eyes. They looked ready to pounce. Pip tried to growl at them, but the pipes in his mouth made the sound come out all wrong. Robbie tried to calm him down. "You're a brave dog, but you're too small to take on those leopards. And in any case, they are only paintings!"

Robbie wondered why there were leopards
painted on the wall. Below them were pictures of people
lying on beds and eating. They seemed to be having a party.
It looked fun. How strange, thought Robbie, it must be very
messy to eat like that ... But Pip wasn't interested in the
painted people. He had heard a noise in the next room.

Robbie found Pip staring at a painting of a man on the wall.
It was Vulca, and he was holding the ball and smiling.
"Good boy, Pip, you've found it!" said Robbie. He grinned
at the painted man. "It was *you* who took my ball!"
So the first mystery was solved, but now there was another
one – how did the ball get into the painting?

Robbie wondered how he could get it back. The painted man
held the ball tightly and smiled, but he didn't say anything. All the
time Pip was barking madly at him. It was his master's ball, and
he wanted it back – *now*! In his excitement he let go of the pipes,
and they fell to the floor. Oh yes, Robbie thought, the pipes ...
Suddenly he had a brilliant idea.

Robbie picked up the pipes and looked at them carefully. They were really odd, nothing like the plastic recorder he played at school. They were shaped like a trumpet, or rather, like two trumpets joined together. Robbie tried blowing into it. *Peep!* No, it was too hard. Pip looked at him curiously. What was Robbie doing with that stick?

Robbie tried again, more gently this time.
The sound that came out was strange,
but strong and sweet. And suddenly the
painted man with the ball moved! First a foot
came out of the wall, then a whole leg, and
then all the rest of him – including Robbie's ball.

The man said, "Hello! I'm Vulca the Etruscan. Well done – you've discovered how to wake us up. If you give me back my pipes, I'll give you back your ball." Robbie did as he was asked. Vulca went on, "I've been living here for two and half thousand years …" He was interrupted by the sound of happy music in the distance. "Come with me!" said Vulca, taking Robbie's hand and leading him outside.

17

"Is it another party?" asked Robbie. "I suppose you could say that,"
Vulca replied. They watched as a long procession of people dressed
in robes passed by. They were carrying vases and flowers and
were dancing and singing. "They're taking a dead person to
his tomb," explained Vulca, "that's our custom."
But Pip was looking at something else ...

"Stop! Where do you think you're going?" shouted
Robbie. Pip was running after a big blue bird that had
flown over his head. Robbie ran after him. Now that
he'd found the ball, he didn't want to lose his dog. Vulca
followed them, smiling to himself. "Children and dogs," he
said, "they never change!" The bird vanished into a hole in

the hillside. Pip went after it, with Robbie and Vulca close behind.
"Stop! Bad dog! Wait for me!" shouted Robbie.
"Let him go," said Vulca, "that bird will lead us to a beautiful tomb."
"*A tomb?*" echoed Robbie in a worried voice, "but that's scary!"
"Why be scared?" smiled Vulca. "You've already been inside a tomb —
the room with the leopards. The whole Necropolis is a cemetery!"

The bird led them into one little room after another. "Isn't that silly bird ever going to stop?" gasped Robbie, out of breath. "Pip must have scared it badly," laughed Vulca. "After all, it's two and a half thousand years old, and it hasn't seen a dog in all that time!"

"Are all of you as old as that?" asked Robbie.

Vulca thought for a moment. "Hmm," he replied, "*Old* isn't quite the right word. Maybe *ancient* ..."

As they spoke the chase became ever more frantic.

At last the blue bird found his friends and they all started flying about crazily in every direction at once. Below them on the walls, fishermen and dolphins were playing among the waves of the painted sea. Vulca sat down and began to play his flute. "You play it much better than I do," admitted Robbie. He looked up at the wall. "And it seems as if they like it too!"

The walls seemed to be full of whirring feathers as the birds' singing blended with Vulca's music. Pip had stopped barking. He was too busy looking at the wall. Those silly birds were flying too high for him to catch them! Robbie, jumping with joy, kicked the ball as hard as he could. Up and up it flew, nearly hitting the ceiling ...

"Oh no! Not again! Give me back my ball!" But it was
no good. Once again the ball had ended up on the wall.
Inside the painting, the fishermen and the dolphins were all
trying to catch it, passing it to each other among the
waves. Some of the men were diving for it, but there was
always a dolphin waiting to hit the ball with its snout

or its tail and then drop it back
into the water, splashing everyone around. There was
no way to get the ball back, so Robbie decided to just enjoy
the show. "This is brilliant!" he said. "It reminds me of
the beach. Look how blue the ocean is!" But Pip was upset.
He couldn't understand why he couldn't join in the fun.

Robbie gave Vulca the ball as a present.
Vulca thanked him. "You're a good boy," he said. "Come back
and see us soon!" Ever since, when tourists come to visit the tombs
in the Necropolis, they are surprised to see Robbie's ball in the
ancient painting. Another Etruscan mystery? Only Robbie,
Pip and Vulca know the secret!

WHO WERE THE ETRUSCANS?

• Tarquinia

Mediterranean Sea

THE ETRUSCANS WERE AN ANCIENT PEOPLE WHO LIVED IN ITALY, MAINLY IN THE AREA OF MODERN TUSCANY AND NORTHERN LAZIO. THE HEIGHT OF ETRUSCAN CIVILIZATION WAS IN THE 7TH AND 6TH CENTURIES BC, WHEN THEIR POWER AND INFLUENCE EXTENDED OVER MUCH OF THE REST OF ITALY.

THE ETRUSCANS OWED THEIR WEALTH LARGELY TO THE MINING AND WORKING OF METALS, WHICH WERE TRADED WITH OTHER PEOPLES IN ITALY AND OVERSEAS, SUCH AS THE PHOENICIANS AND THE GREEKS. THE ETRUSCANS ALSO HAD ABUNDANT HARVESTS OF CORN, OIL AND WINE. WHEN THE ANCIENT ROMANS BECAME STRONG AND POWERFUL THEY EVENTUALLY CONQUERED THE ETRUSCANS, BUT THE ROMANS LEARNED AND COPIED MUCH FROM THEM.

• Etruria, the land of the Etruscans, was a collection of city states – in other words, self-governing, independent communities. Each of those communities was ruled by a **lucumo**, who was a kind of local king and religious ruler. We

know a lot about the wealthy families who were buried in elaborate tombs, sometimes with many possessions or gifts, but far less about the poorer people – the peasants, laborers, mine-workers and slaves.

• Like many ancient peoples, Etruscans were deeply interested in foretelling the future. **Augurs** were priests who predicted the future by watching and interpreting the flight of birds in the

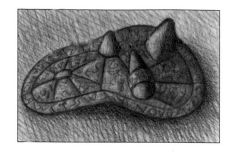

sky. **Haruspices** killed animals and tried to "see" the will of the gods by examining the internal organs of the animals, particularly the **liver**. The picture above shows a bronze model of a liver, probably used for training priests.

• Most of our knowledge of the Etruscans comes from their **necropoleis**, (cemeteries, literally "cities of the dead"). Many of these cemeteries have been excavated by archaeologists, or, less happily, dug up by tomb robbers. The cemeteries are usually easier to study than the remains of Etruscan towns, since

later cities have often been built over the same sites as the Etruscan ones. Some of the most famous cemeteries are those of Tarquinia, where our story is set.

In a necropolis, the insides of the tombs were built to look like the houses of the living, because the Eruscans believed that there was life after death. They sometimes buried their loved ones with their own belongings, including pottery, bronze vessels, arms and armor, mirrors and jewelry. All these things, and the frescoes

painted on the walls of the tombs, help us to imagine what their daily life must have been like.

• The Etruscan language has now been largely deciphered, thanks to the efforts of scholars. It is written in an alphabet

based on the ancient Greek letters. The examples of Etruscan writing that survive, however, are mostly short inscriptions on burial containers. They only tell us the name and age of the dead person.

• The Etruscans often built their cities on top of steep hills. They were excellent engineers and architects, and could build solid and elegant stone arches. Traces of their architecture can even be found in Rome, which at one time is said to have been ruled by Etruscan kings. The Etruscans drained marshy land, making it cultivable, and dug channels to irrigate their fields.

• Rich and fashionable Etruscans wore much gold jewelry, which was exquisitely made: rings,

brooches, bracelets, necklaces, and hair-ornaments. Occasionally they wore a diadem, a headdress like a tiara. Women wore elaborate tunics, cloaks, and sometimes distinctive boots or slippers with turned-up toes.

• The Etruscan people particularly loved music, dancing, boxing, athletics and wrestling. Sports (including running, the long jump, discus and javelin-throwing) took place on special days, when animals were sacrificed to secure the favor of the gods. Other favorite sports were horse racing and chariot racing.

• The Etruscans believed in many gods. We can see images of them on painted pottery, bronze statuettes, terracotta statues and engravings on the backs of bronze mirrors. Gods were shown in human form; they were believed to rule the heavens, the earth and nature.